Classic Cocktail Guides
and Retro Bartender Books

One Hundred and One Drinks As They Are Mixed

Recipes for Cocktails and Other Beverages Served During Prohibition

Originally Distributed by Kuenzle & Streiff, Manila, Philippines

Historic Cookbooks of the World
Kalevala Books, Chicago

"The proper union of gin and vermouth is a great and sudden glory; it is one of the happiest marriages on earth, and one of the shortest lived."
— Bernard DeVoto (1897–1955)

One Hundred and One Drinks As They Are Mixed:
Recipes for Cocktails and Other Beverages Served During Prohibition

Joanne Asala, Editor
Historic Cookbooks of the World

Rowan Grier, Series Editor
Classic Cocktail Guides
and Retro Bartender Books

Classic Cocktail Guides and Retro Bartender Books and *Historic Cookbooks of the World* are published by Kalevala Books, an imprint of Compass Rose Technologies, Inc., PO Box 409095, Chicago, IL 60640. Titles published by Kalevala Books are available at special quantity discounts to use as premiums and sales promotions or for academic use. For more information, please write to the Director of Special Sales, Compass Rose Technologies, Inc., PO Box 409095, Chicago, IL 60640 or contact us through our Web site, www.CompassRose.com.

Editors' Note

Some ingredients found in vintage cocktail guides are unavailable or hard to come by today. Check out our resource guide at the back for vendors who specialize in hard-to-find ingredients and websites with information on how to recreate classic cocktails and cocktail ingredients.

ISBN: 978-1-880954-42-3

Historic Cookbooks of the World

Historic Cookbooks of the World

HAUT-SAUTERNES

A
Chilled
Bottle of
Haut-
Sauterne
Adds Zest
to any
Dinner

HAUT-SAUTERNES

ED. KRESSMANN & Cº
BORDEAUX

KUENZLE & STREIFF, Inc.

SOLE DISTRIBUTORS

PHONE 113   343 T. PINPIN

CANADIAN CLUB
RYE WHISKY

For years
the formost

Rye Whisky

❦

The best
Whisky for
High Balls

KUENZLE & STREIFF, Inc.
SOLE DISTRIBUTORS

PHONE 113　　　　　　　　　　**343 T. PINPIN**

Foreword

This Book was prepared at the request of our friends and the customers who would serve the proper mixed drinks prepared in the right manner.

We should, therefore, like to emphasise the fact that, to obtain the desired results, GORDON'S DRY GIN and other products should be used as mentioned. No other brands would be "just as good."

When calling for your favorite cocktail at your Club, Hotel, or Restaurant, always specify "With Gordon's Gin," and when ordering Gin from your dealer, specify "GORDON'S" and see that you get it.

1

How often have you wished
for a good cup of Coffee?

Take Home a Trial can of

SCHILLING'S
C O F F E E

Tonight and realize your wish

KUENZLE & STREIFF, Inc.

SOLE DISTRIBUTORS

PHONE 113   343 T. PINPIN

HOW TO SERVE A GOOD COCKTAIL

First. The ingredients must be of the best quality. Where it calls for GIN use "GORDONS."

Second. The glass used in serving should be sufficiently large to serve a generous COCKTAIL and not be more than three-quarters full.

Third. All cocktail glasses should be chilled before filling and serving.

Fourth. In case a Cocktail-shaker is not available, a large glass or tumbler, will serve, if the ingredients are well stirred.

WHISKY COBBLER

Use large mixing glass, filled with fine ice, add one half teaspoonful of sugar, one and one half teaspoonfuls of Pineapple syrup, one half wine glass of ISUAN, one wine glass of ROBERTSON'S WHISKY, stir well with spoon, and ornament top with sliced orange and serve with straw.

GIN SLING

Fill half pint tumbler with chipped ice, put in two teaspoonfuls of sugar, juice of half Lemon, add half wine glassful of GORDON'S DRY GIN and fill with soda water. Stir well.

LONG DRINK

Use large glass add piece of ice, one wine glass of GORDON'S DRY GIN, long winding piece of Grape-fruit or Lemon peel—and serve.

TRINIDAD PUNCH

Into one pint of GORDON'S FINEST JAMAICA RUM dissolve one stick of Vanilla; when well mixed, strain; add two pints of Cocoanut Milk. This punch may be served either hot or cold.

FIFTY FIFTY COCKTAIL

Fill shaker half full with cracked ice, add fifty per cent GORDON'S DRY GIN, fifty per cent French Vermouth, shake well—serve in small glass—very cold.

NATURES
BEST

MINERAL
WATER

SHERRY WINE EGG NOGG

Use large shaker filled with fine ice, add one fresh egg, one half table-spoonful of sugar, one wine glass of Sherry wine, one pony of Hennessy's Brandy, shake well until thoroughly mixed, strain into fancy glass, grate nutmeg on top and serve.

SHERRY WINE PUNCH

Use large mixing glass filled with fine shaved ice, one half glass of Grenadine syrup, one dash of lemon juice, one and one half glasses Sherry wine, stir well and top it off with Claret Wine, serve with straw.

STONE FENCE

Use whisky glass with two or three lumps of ice, add one wine glass of Bourbon Whisky, fill glass with cider, stir well and serve.

TOM COLLINS

Use extra large mixing glass, add three or four lumps of broken ice, one wine glass of GORDON'S OLD TOM GIN, one bottle of Isuan, one half liqueur glass of Benedictine, mix well and serve, this drink must be drunk while effervecing.

VANILLA PUNCH

Use large mixing glass, filled with shaved ice, add two or three dashes of lemon juice, two or three dashes of

Curacoa dissolved in water, one pony of Hennessy's brandy, one and one half wine glasses of Vanilla, mix well with spoon and serve with piece of sliced pineapple.

JOHN COLLINS

Fill large mixing glass half full of cracked ice, add one teaspoonful of sugar, three dashes of lemon juice, one jigger of GORDON'S OLD TOM GIN, one bottle of ISUAN, stir well and serve while effervecing.

TOM AND JERRY
(*How to prepare*)

Separate the yolks from the whites of three eggs; beat the white to a stiff froth and stirr the yolks to a very thin mixture; mix together in a Tom and Jerry bowl and stir in fine sugar until you have a medium stiff batter.

TOM AND JERRY
(*How to serve*)

Use Tom and Jerry mug, fill mug one fourth full of batter, one half jigger of GORDON'S JAMAICA RUM, one half jigger of Hennessy's Brandy, mix well with small spoon; fill with hot water; stir again; sprinkle nutmeg on top and serve.

ROMAN PUNCH

Use large mixing glass, add one half tablespoonful of sugar, one half pony raspberry syrup, two or three dashes of lemon juice, one fourth pony Curacao, one half wine glass Hennessy's Brandy, one half pony GORDON'S JAM-AICA RUM, stir well with spoon, garnish top with cherry or pineapple and serve with straw.

GOLDEN FIZZ

Fill large shaker with fine ice, add one half tablespoon-ful of sugar, four dashes of lemon juice, one wine glass of GORDON'S OLD TOM GIN, the yolk of one fresh egg, shake well; strain into fizz glass, and fill with ISUAN and serve to be drunk while effervescing.

ABSINTHE FRAPPE

Use large shaker filled with shaved ice, one teaspoon-ful of Benedictine, one pony of Absinthe, one wine glass of water, shake well until outside of shaker is frosted and serve.

HORSE'S NECK

Use large fizz glass with three lumps of ice, add lemon peel of one whole lemon cut in one long string and ar-ranged in glass, allowing one end to hang over the edge of the glass. Fill glass with ISUAN PALE GINGER ALE and serve.

MINT JULEP

Use large glass with mint leaves crushed in the bot-tom, add one tablespoonful of sugar, one jigger of Cognac, one dash of Jamaica Rum, stir well and fill glass with shaved ice, dress with a few sprigs of mint leaves moist-ened and dipped in sugar, served with straws.

TUXEDO COCKTAIL

Fill mixing glass with fine ice, add one dash of Angostura bitters, one fourth glass of Sherry wine, one jigger of Italian Vermouth, "Cinzano," three fourths jigger of GORDON'S OLD TOM GIN, mix well, serve in cocktail glass, very cold.

MANILA COCKTAIL

Use large mixing glass filled with ice, add one wine glass of French Vermouth, one wine glass of GORDON'S OLD TOM GIN, shake well and serve in cocktail glass with twisted orange peel on top.

ARMY AND NAVY COCKTAIL

Use large mixing glass filled with ice, add three dashes of Angostura bitters, one teaspoonful of sugar, one pony of Italian Vermouth, "Cinzano," one and one half ponies of Hennessy's Brandy, mix well and serve in cocktail glass with dash of ISUAN on top.

SILVER FIZZ

Fill large mixing glass with cracked ice, add one half teaspoonful of sugar, one fourth wine glass of lemon juice, one jigger of GORDON'S OLD TOM GIN, white of one egg, shake well, strain and serve in fizz glass, fill up glass with ISUAN.

MORNING GLORY FIZZ

Use mixing glass with two or three lumps of ice, add one heaping tablespoonful of sugar, juice of, one lemon, one wine glass of GORDON'S OLD TOM GIN, two dashes of Absinthe, white of one egg, shake well and serve in large punch glass, fill glass with ISUAN and serve, to be drunk while effervescing.

VERMOUTH COCKTAIL

Fill large mixing glass three fourths with shave ice, add two or three dashes of bitters, one wine glass of French Vermouth, one wine glass of Italian Vermouth, "Cinzano," two dashes of Maraschino, stir well with spoon; strain into cocktail glass, twist lemon peel on top and serve.

VIRGIN COCKTAIL

Fill mixing glass half full of cracked ice, add two dashes of Angostura Bitters, two dashes of raspberry syrup, one half jigger of French Vermouth, one half jigger of GORDON'S OLD TOM GIN, stir well and serve very cold.

WHISKY COCKTAIL

Fill large mixing glass with shaved ice, add two or three dashes of bitters, two teaspoonfuls of sugar, one or two dashes of Curacoa, one wine glass of CANADIAN CLUB WHISKY, stir well and serve with piece of lemon peel.

WHITE ROSE COCKTAIL

Half fill mixing glass with cracked ice, add one half measure of GORDON'S DRY GIN, one quarter measure of Anisette, white of one egg, one spoonful of pure cream, shake well and strain into cocktail glass.

USE
LEMOS LEMON JUICE
IN YOUR MIXED DRINKS

Pure Lemon Juice

with the

True Fruit

Flavor.

—

Will not Spoil

When

Opened

KUENZLE & STREIFF, Inc.

SOLE DISTRIBUTORS

PHONE 113   343 T. PINPIN

PINK LADY COCKTAIL

Fill shaker quarter full with cracked ice, pour in one fresh egg well beaten, add four dashes of bitters, three fourths glass of lemon juice, three fourths glass of Grenadine syrup, five drops of Absinthe, one and one half glasses GORDON'S SLOE GIN, one half glass GORDON'S OLD TOM GIN, one and one half French Vermouth, shake well and serve in chilled glasses.

SARATOGA COCKTAIL

Fill shaker half full of cracked ice, one tablespoonful sugar, two or three slices of orange, two jiggers of sherry, two dashes of Angostura Bitters, shake well and fill up glass with ice.

SILVER COCKTAIL

Use mixing glass half full of ice, add two dashes of GORDON'S ORANGE BITTERS, one half teaspoonful Angostura bitters, two dashes of Maraschino, one half jigger of French Vermouth, one half jigger of GORDON'S OLD TOM GIN, stir well and serve in cocktail glass, twist lemon peel on top and serve.

SUNSHINE COCKTAIL

Fill mixing glass with cracked ice, add one third measure French Vermouth, one third measure Italian Vermouth, "Cinzano," one third measure GORDON'S DRY GIN, stir until very cold and pour into cocktail glass and serve with twisted orange peel on top.

MARTINI COCKTAIL

Fill mixing glass with cracked ice, add two or three dashes of Bitters, two third wine glass of GORDON'S DRY GIN, one third glass of French or Italian Vermouth, stir well with spoon and strain into cocktail glass, and squeeze piece of lemon peel on top.

MERRY WIDOW COCKTAIL

Fill shaker with cracked ice, add one pony of Maraschino, one half pony Italian Vermouth "Cinzano," one pony French Vermouth, shake well and serve with cherry.

MILLION DOLLAR COCKTAIL

Fill shaker two thirds full of cracked ice, two dashes of Grenadine syrup, two dashes pineapple juice, one half wine glass GORDON'S OLD TOM GIN, one half glass of French Vermouth, white of an egg, shake well and serve with small piece of pineapple.

OLD TOM GIN COCKTAIL

Use mixing glass filled with fine ice, add one dash of Angostura bitters, two dashes of Curacao, one wine glass of GORODN'S OLD TOM GIN, stir well and serve with a piece of twisted lemon peel on top.

OLD FASHIONED COCKTAIL

Use mixing glass half full of cracked ice, add one lump of sugar, one or two dashes of bitters, one dash of GORDON'S ORANGE BITTERS, one dash of Angostura bitters, lemon peel one piece, one jigger of CANADIAN CLUB WHISKY, add ISUAN and stir gently with spoon and serve.

Buchanan's
Liqueur Scotch Whisky

Finest Quality in Scotch

KUENZLE & STREIFF, Inc.

SOLE DISTRIBUTORS

PHONE 113   343 T. PINPIN

HONGKONG COCKTAIL

Fill shaker with cracked ice, add one teaspoonful of sugar, one tablespoon of Lime juice, one third measure of GORDON'S GIN, one third measure of French Vermouth, one third measure of Orange juice, five drops Angostura bitters, shake well, strain and serve in cocktail glass.

IRISH COCKTAIL

Fill large mixing glass with shaved ice, add two dashes of Absinthe, one dash Maraschino, one dash Curacao, two dashes GORDON'S OLD TOM GIN, one wine glass of Irish Whisky, stir well with spoon, after straining in cocktail glass, put in small olive and squeeze lemon peel.

JAPANESE COCKTAIL

Use large mixing glass three-fourths, full of cracked ice, add two or three dashes Grenadine syrup two or three dashes bitters, one glass of Bacardi, two dashes of Maraschino, mix well with a spoon and strain into cocktail glass and twist a piece of lemon peel on top, and serve.

MANHATTAN COCKTAIL

Fill mixing glass with cracked ice, add one or two dashes of bitters, one dash of Curacao, one half wine glass of CANADIAN CLUB WHISKY, one half wine glass of Italian Vermouth "Cinzano," stir well and strain into a cocktail glass, twist a piece of lemon peel on top, serve.

CHERRY BRANDY COCKTAIL

Angostura bitters, one wine glass of Cherry Brandy, one wine glass of GORDON'S DRY GIN, two dashes of

GORDON'S ORANGE BITTERS, pour into shaker filled with cracked ice, shake well and serve in cocktail glass.

ROBERTSON'S COCKTAIL

Fill shaker with cracked ice, add one fourth wine glass of ROBERTSON'S WHISKY, one fourth glass CANADIAN CLUB WHISKY, one fourth glass of Brandy, shake well and serve in a chilled glass.

GIBSON COCKTAIL

Into mixing glass well filled with ice, add one half measure of GORDON'S DRY GIN, one half measure of French Vermouth, stir well, strain and serve.

EAST INDIA COCKTAIL

Use large mixing glass filled with shaved ice, one teaspoon of Curacao, one teaspoon of pineapple syrup, two or three dashed of bitters, two dashes of Maraschino, one wine glass of Brandy, stir well, strain into cocktail glasses, twist a piece of lemon peel on top and serve.

HONOLULU COCKTAIL

Use champagne glass and add one small piece of ice, two dashes of Angostura bitters, one jigger of ROBERTSON'S WHISKY, fill glass with ISUAN, then drop in a small spoon of sugar and stir; drink while effervescing.

CHAMPAGNE COCKTAIL

Place two or three small lumps of crystal ice in the bottom of a Champagne glass and mix as follows: One

GORDON'S
READY MIXED COCKTAILS

When your
Friends Drop in
Unexpectedly
at Cocktail Time

GORDON'S
Ready Mixed
Cocktails

are just the right
thing

No trouble or
Bother

They come ready
to serve

KUENZLE & STREIFF, Inc.
SOLE DISTRIBUTORS
PHONE 113   343 T. PINPIN

Classic Cocktail Guides and Retro Bartender Books

slice of Orange placed on ice, one square of Pineapple, one lump of cube sugar placed on ice, two or three dashes of Bitters fill glasses with Charles Heidseick Champagne.

CLUB COCKTAIL

Half glass of cracked ice, two dashes of GORDON'S OLD TOM GIN, one third glass Italian Vermouth "Cinzano," two dashes of GORDON'S ORANGE BITTERS, one dash Green Chartreuse, stir well and serve—very cold.

CLOVER COCKTAIL

Fill shaker with cracked ice and add one third wine glass French Vermouth, two thirds wine glass GORDON'S DRY GIN, one teaspoon of lemon juice, three teaspoons of Grenadine syrup, white of one egg, shake well, strain and serve.

COFFEE COCKTAIL

Place three or four lumps of ice in a mixing glass, add one teaspoonful of sugar, one fresh egg, one glass of Port Wine, one pony glass of Brandy, shake well and strain into punch glass with a little nutmeg on top.

DESPEDIDA COCKTAIL

Juice of two lemons, two wine glass of Bacardi, one wine glass of GORDON'S DRY GIN, one half wine glass French Vermouth, one half wine glass of Heering's Brandy.

ANGEL KISS COCKTAIL

Use Liqueur glass, one fourth Grenadine, one fourth Creme de Cacao, one fourth milk, one fourth Heering's Brandy.

Classic Cocktail Guides and Retro Bartender Books

BARRY COCKTAIL

Use small glass and piece of ice, two dashes of Angostura Bitters, one half jigger of GORDON'S DRY GIN, one jigger of Italian Vermouth "Cinzano," one piece of twisted lemon peel, five drops of Creme de Menthe, stir well and strain into small glasses and serve.

BIJOU COCKTAIL

Three quarters of a glass filled with shaved ice, one third wine glass Green Chartreuse, one third wine glass Italian Vermuoth "Cinzano," one third wine glass GORDON'S OLD TOM GIN, stir well and after straining into cocktail glass, add cherry or small olive, and serve after squeezing lemon peel on top.

DAISY GIN COCKTAIL

Fill pint shaker with cracked ice, add one half wine glass of raspberry syrup or Grenadine, one half wine glass GORDON'S DRY GIN, one tablespoon of lemon juice, two slices orange, two lumps of sugar, shake well and serve.

ORANGE BLOSSOM COCKTAIL

Fill shaker with cracked ice, one half glass GORDON'S DRY GIN, juice of one half orange, shake well and serve in small glass—very cold.

21

CHARLES HEIDSEICK

THE KING OF

CHAMPAGNE

*No Banquet, Dinner or Party is
complete without it*

KUENZLE & STREIFF, Inc.

SOLE DISTRIBUTORS

PHONE 113   **343 T. PINPIN**

22

CLOVER CLUB COCKTAIL

Fill shaker half full with chipped ice, add fifty per cent GORDON'S DRY GIN, fifty per cent French Vermouth, shake well—serve in small glass—very cold.

BRONX COCKTAIL

Fill shaker half full with cracked ice, squeeze the juice of a quarter of an orange into shaker, add one third GORDON'S DRY GIN, one third Italian Vermouth "Cinzano," and one third French Vermouth, shake well—serve in small glass—very cold.

GORDON'S GIN COCKTAIL

Fill shaker with chipped ice, wine glassful GORDON'S DRY GIN, few drops Angostura bitters, few drops plain syrup, shake well—serve in small glass—very cold, with small piece of lemon peel.

DUBONNET COCKTAIL

Fill shaker with chipped ice, add one third GORDON'S DRY GIN, two thirds Dubonnet, shake well—serve in small glass—very cold.

PERFECT COCKTAIL

Fill shaker with cracked ice, one half wine glass GORDON'S DRY GIN, one fourth wine glass French Vermouth, one fourth wine glass Italian Vermouth, "Cinzano," shake well—serve in small glass—very cold.

TROPICAL COCKTAIL

Fill shaker with cracked ice, add wine glass of GORDON'S DRY GIN, wine glass of orange juice or grape juice, shake well—serve in small glasses—very cold.

FANCY BRANDY SMASH

Use large mixing glass one half full of ice, add one half tablespoonful of sugar, one half glass ISUAN, three or four sprigs of mint well dissolved, one wine glass of Hennessy's Brandy, mix well and serve in fancy glass.

FANCY BRANDY SMASH

Use a large bar glass, one half tablespoonful of sugar, one half glass of ISUAN, three or four sprigs of fresh mint, dissolved well, one half glass of shaved ice, one wine glass of Hennessy's Brandy, stir up well with a spoon, strain into a fancy bar glass.

FANCY BRANDY SOUR

Use a large bar glass, one half tablespoonful of sugar, two or three dashes of lemon juice, one squirt of ISUAN water, dissolve the sugar and lemon well with a spoon, fill up the glass with ice, one wine glass of Hennessy's Brandy, stir up well, place the fruits into the fancy sour glass, strain the ingredients into it, and serve.

FANCY WHISKY SMASH

Use a large bar glass, one half tablespoonful of sugar, one half glass of water, or ISUAN, three or four sprigs of

Classic Cocktail Guides and Retro Bartender Books

mint, dissolve well with a spoon, fill the glass of fine shaved ice, one wine glass of Canadian Club Whisky, stir up well with a spoon; strain it into a fancy sour glass, and serve; this drink requires particular care and attention, so as to have it palatable and look proper.

FEDORA

Use a large bar glass, one pony of Hennessy's Brandy, one pony of Curacao, one half pony of Bacardi rum, one half pony of Canadian Club, one tablespoonful of powdered sugar, dissolve in a little water, one slice of lemon; fill the tumbler with fine ice, shake well and ornament with berries or small pieces of orange, serve with a straw.

GIN COASTER

Use large glass, add one third GORDON'S OLD TOM GIN, dash of GORDON'S ORANGE BITTERS, fill up glass with ISUAN, add ice.

LEAVE IT TO ME

Fill shaker with chipped ice, put in half teaspoonful of powdered sugar, squeeze half lemon in, add a teaspoonful of raspberry syrup and one of Maraschino, half a wine glass of GORDON'S OLD TOM GIN, shake well and strain into a small glass, place a slice of lemon on top and serve.

"CUILER'S" RUM PUNCH

One bottle of Hennessy's Brandy, one pint of GORDON'S FINEST JAMAICA RUM, one half pint of Sherry, juice of three lemons, a little grated nutmeg, lemon peel, one quart of boiling water, put the thin paring of two lemons into a mortar with half pound of sugar, beat into a mass, strain the lemon juice and add, mix well and put the ingredient into a jug, then add the sherry, rum, brandy and lastly the boiling water, in one quarter of an hour the drink will be ready.

BIANCO COCKTAIL

Use large shaker filled with cracked ice, add three drops of Angostura bitters, one third GORDON'S MARTINI, two thirds measure of CANADIAN CLUB WHISKEY, shake well and serve in cocktail glass.

DAMSON GIN COCKTAIL

Fill shaker with chipped ice, add sixty per cent GORDON'S DAMSON GIN, thirty per cent GORDON'S DRY GIN, ten per cent GORDON'S ORANGE BITTERS, shake well—serve in small glass—very cold.

GIN RICKEY

Use large glass, add one lump of ice, juice of half lime, wine glass of GORDON'S DRY GIN, fill up glass with ISUAN.

HOT GIN TODDY FOR COLDS

Take tumbler, put in wine glass GORDON'S DRY GIN, juice of one lemon and add sugar to taste, fill glass up with hot water and drink immediately before retiring.

IMPERIAL
BLACKBERRY BRANDY

An Ideal Tonic for Stomache and Indigestion, made from the choicest Blackberries and French Brandy

A Delightful after Dinner Drink

KUENZLE & STREIFF, Inc.
SOLE DISTRIBUTORS

PHONE 113   343 T. PINPIN

27

MERRY WIDOW COCKTAIL

Use large shaker three fourth full of cracked ice, add one pony of Maraschino, one half pony of GORDON'S MARTINI, one pony of French Vermouth, shake well and serve with cherry.

SARATOGA COCKTAIL

Use large shaker half full of ice, add one tablespoonful of sugar, two slices of orange, two jiggers of Sherry wine, two dashes Angostura bitters, shake well and serve with small onion.

ANGLERS COCKTAIL

Fill a shaker with chipped ice, put in two or three drops of Angostura bitters, half a teaspoonful of GORDON'S ORANGE BITTERS, and three or four drops of raspberry syrup, add half wine glass full of GORDON'S DRY GIN, shake well and serve in a small glass—very cold.

SLOE GIN COCKTAIL

Fill shaker with chipped ice, add one third GORDON'S SLOE GIN, one third GORDON'S DRY GIN, one third French Vermouth, one dash of lemon juice, shake well—serve in small glass—very cold.

TURF COCKTAIL

Use large mixing glass, half full of ice, add two dashes of Absinthe, two dashes Maraschino, two dashes GORDON'S ORANGE BITTERS, two dashes of Angostura

Classic Cocktail Guides and Retro Bartender Books

bitters, one half jigger Vermouth, one half jigger GOR-
DON'S OLD TOM GIN, stir well, strain into cocktail glass
and serve, an olive may be added if desired.

McGREGOR EGG NOGG

Use large bar glass, add yolk of one fresh egg, three
fourths tablespoonful of sugar, add a little nutmeg and
cinnamon, beat to a cream, one half glass, HENNESSY'S
BRANDY, one fourth pony GORDON'S JAMAICA RUM,
one wine glass of Sherry wine, fill glass with milk, shake
well, strain into large bar glass, grate a little nutmeg on
top.

LEAP FROG COCKTAIL

Use cocktail shaker, add two or three lumps of ice, one
or two dashes of lemon juice, one half wine glass of Grenadine, one half wine glass of Apricot Brandy, one half
glass GORDON'S JAMAICA RUM, shake well and serve
in wine glass.

GOLDEN SLIPPERS

One half wine glass Chartreuse, yolk of one egg, one
half wine glass of Heering's Cherry Brandy; this drink
must be mixed in a careful manner so that the yolk of
the egg does not run into the liquor.

WHISKEY COBBLER

Use large mixing glass, add one half tablespoonful of
sugar, one and one half teaspoonfuls of pineapple syrup,

Mount Blanc
French Vermouth

The Perfect
**FRENCH
VERMOUTH**

for Cocktails

and other

Mixed

Beverages

KUENZLE & STREIFF, Inc.

SOLE DISTRIBUTORS

PHONE 113   343 T. PINPIN

Classic Cocktail Guides and Retro Bartender Books

one half wine glass of ISUAN dissolve well with spoon, fill up glass with fine ice, one wine glass of ROBERTSON'S WHISKEY, stir well with spoon and ornament the top with orange serve with straw.

WHISKEY CRUSTA

Peel one lemon and fit it into a cocktail glass so as to cover the entire glass, then moisten the glass with a piece of lemon and dip the glass into powdered sugar. Make the following mixture: use large mixing glass, add one half glass of shaved ice, four dashes of gum syrup, two dashes of Angostura bitters, two dashes of lemon juice, two dashes of Curacao, one jigger of CANADIAN CLUB WHISKEY, stir well with spoon and poor into glass prepared with lemon peel and serve.

WHISKEY DAISY

Use small bar glass, and fill glass one half full with fine ice, three or four dashes of gum syrup, two or three dashes of Curacao, juice from one half lemon, orange bitters two or three dashes, one wine glass of CANADIAN CLUB WHISKEY, shake well and fill glass with ISUAN and serve.

WHISKEY FIZZ

Use large mixing glass, add one teaspoonful of sugar, two or three dashes of lemon juice, one squirt of ISUAN, one wine glass of ROBERTSON'S WHISKEY, stir well and strain into a good sized fizz glass, fill up balance with ISUAN and serve. This drink should be drank while effervescing.

WHISKEY JULEP

Use large mixing glass, add three fourths tablespoonful of sugar, one half wine glass of ISUAN, three or four sprigs of fresh mint, fill glass with shaved ice, one wine glass of CANADIAN CLUB WHISKEY, stir up well with a spoon and ornament the top with mint, oranges, pineapples, sprinkle a little sugar on top. Add a dash of GORDON'S JAMAICA RUM on top.

WHISKEY SOUR

Use large mixing glass, add one half table spoonful of sugar, three or four dashes of lemon juice, one squirt of ISUAN, one wine glass of CANADIAN CLUB WHISKEY, fill glass with fine ice stir well and serve.

GIN SMASH

Use large mixing glass, add one half tablespoonful of sugar, two or three sprigs of French mint, dissolve well with a little water until the essence of the mint is extracted, one half glass of shaved ice, one wine glass of GORDON'S DRY GIN, stir well with spoon, strain into glass and ornament with small piece of orange.

GIN SOUR

Use large bar glass, add one or two lumps of broken ice, one wine glass of GORDON'S DRY GIN, one dash of lime juice, one squirt of ISUAN, fill glass with three fourths fine ice, mix well and strain into glass and serve with a little pineapple on top.

Historic Cookbooks of the World

GIN TODDY

Use whiskey glass, add one half teaspoonful of sugar, two or three lumps of ice, one wine glass of GORDON'S DRY GIN, stir well with spoon and serve.

COLD WHISKEY SLING

Use large mixing glass, add one teaspoonful of sugar, one half wine glass water, one or two lumps of ice, one wine glass of CANADIAN CLUB WHISKEY, mix well and grate a little nutmeg on top, and serve.

CURACAO PUNCH

Use large mixing glass, add one half tablespoonful of sugar, two or three dashes of lemon juice, one half wine glass water, fill glass with shaved ice, one half wine glass of Hennessy's Brandy, one wine glass of Curacao, one half pony of GORDON'S JAMAICA RUM, stir well and serve with straw.

EGG LEMONADE

Use large shaker, add one fresh egg, one tablespoonful of sugar, eight dashes of lemon juice, three fourths glass fine ice, fill up shaker with ISUAN, shake well and strain into large glass.

EGG MILK PUNCH

Use large shaker, add one fresh egg, three fourths spoonful of sugar, one fourth wine glass of shaved ice, one wine glass of Hennessy's Brandy, one pony of GORDON'S JAMAICA RUM, fill up balance with milk, shake well until the ingredients become a stiff cream, strain into large glass and grate a little nutmeg on top and serve.

EGG NOGG

Use shaker, add one fresh egg, three fourths table-spoonful of sugar, one third wine glass of ice, one pony glass of GORDON'S JAMAICA RUM, one wine glass of Hennessy's Brandy, fill up balance of glass with milk, shake well until ingredients are well mixed.

SHERIDAN FLIP

Use large bar glass, add one fresh egg, three-fourths tablespoonful of sugar, three fourths glass of shaved ice, one wine glass of Hennessy's Brandy, shake well, and strain into fancy glass, grate a little nutmeg on top and serve.

SHERRY COBBLER

Use large bar glass, add one tablespoonful of sugar, three pieces of twisted lemon peel, fill glass with fine ice, fill glass nearly to top with Sherry wine, stir well bring the lemon peel nearly to the top, dress with fruit in season and serve with straw.

SLOE GIN FIZZ

Use large cocktail shaker, add one half glass of fine ice, three dashes of lemon juice, one half tablespoonful of sugar, one jigger of GORDON'S SLOE GIN, shake well and strain into a fizz glass, fill glass with ISUAN and serve, to be drunk while effervescing.

MISSISSIPPI PUNCH

Use large shaker, add one tablespoonful of sugar, one half glass of ISUAN, two dashes of lemon juice, one half wine glass of GORDON'S JAMAICA RUM, one half wine glass of CANADIAN CLUB WHISKEY, one wine glass of HENNESSY'S BRANDY, fill glass with fine ice, shake well and serve with straw.

SATINAS POUSSE CAFE

Use a Sherry wine glass, one third wine glass of Maraschino, one third wine glass of Curacao (red), one third wine glass of Hennessy's Brandy, and serve. This drink is generally indulged in after partaking of a cup of black coffee, and care must be taken to prevent the different liquors from running into each other, as the proper appearance has a great deal to do with it.

SAUTERNE COBBLER

Use a large bar glass, one half tablespoonful of sugar, one half wine glass syrup, one fourth glass ISUAN, dissolved well with a spoon, fill the glass with fine shaved ice, one and one half wine glass of Sauterne wine, stir up well, and serve with a straw.

PORT WINE PUNCH

One glass full of fine ice, one half tablespoonful of sugar, one tablespoonful of syrup, one or two dashes of lemon juice, one half wine glass full of water, dissolve well with sugar and lemon, fill up the glass with Port wine, mix well with a spoon and serve with a straw.

PORT WINE SANGAREE

Use a small bar glass, one teaspoonful of sugar, dissolve well with a little water, one or two lumps of ice, one

36

Classic Cocktail Guides and Retro Bartender Books

wine glass of Port wine, stir up with a spoon, remove the piece of ice if required, grate a little nutmeg on top, and serve.

BRANDY DAISY

Use a large bar glass, one half tablespoonful of sugar, two or three dashes of lemon juice, one squirt ISUAN, dissolve well with a spoon, one half glass of Chartreuse (yellow), fill up the glass with fine ice, one glass of Hennessy's Brandy, stir up well with a spoon place into a fancy bar glass, and serve.

BRANDY PUNCH

Use a large bar glass, three fourths tablespoonful of sugar, a few drops of pineapple syrup, one or two dashes of lemon juice, one squirt of ISUAN, dissolve with a spoon, fill up the glass, with finely shaved ice, one and one half glassful of Hennessy's Brandy, stir up well, flavor with a few drops of Bacardi rum, and serve with a straw.

BACARDI RUM PUNCH

Use a large bar glass, one tablespoonful of sugar, three or four dashes of lemon juice, one half wine glass of water, dissolve well, one fourth pony glass of GORDON'S rum, one wine glass of Bacardi rum, fill up with fine shaved ice, mix well with a spoon, and serve with a straw. This is very cooling and pleasant drink in the tropics.

BRANDY SANGAREE

Use a small bar glass, one or two lumps of ice, one half wine glass of water, one half tablespoonful of sugar, one

37

glass of Hennessy's Brandy, stir up well with a spoon, grate a little nutmeg on top, and serve, strain if desired.

BRANDY FIX

Use a large bar glass, one half tablespoonful of sugar, two or three dashes of lemon juice, one half pony glass of pineapple syrup, one or two dashes of Chartreuse (green), dissolve well with a little ISUAN, fill up the glass with shaved ice, one wine glass of Hennessy's Brandy, stir up with a spoon and serve with a straw.

BRANDY FIZZ

Use a large bar glass, one half tablespoonful of sugar, three or four dashes of lemon juice, three fourths of a glass of fine ice, one wine glass of Hennessy's Brandy, mix well with a spoon, strain into a fizz or sour glass fill with ISUAN and serve.

CHAMPAGNE COBBLER

Use a large bar glass, one fourth of a tablespoonful of sugar, one fourth wine glass of ISUAN, dissolve well, one or two pieces of orange, one or two pieces of pineapple, fill the glass with ice, fill the balance with Charles Heidseick Champagne, and serve it with a straw.

CHAMPAGNE CUP

One quart Charles Heidseick Champagne, two bottles ISUAN soda, one half Sherry-glass Sherry, one half Liqueur glass Hennessy's Brandy, add six cherries, few slices pineapple, few slices fresh lemon, ice.

CHAMPAGNE SOUR

Use fancy glass, one lump of loaf sugar, two dashes of fresh lemon juice, place the saturated sugar into a fancy glass, also a slice of orange and a slice of pineapple, fill up the glass slowly with Charles Heidseick Champagne, and stir up well, and serve.

CHAMPAGNE VELVET

Use a large size goblet, for this drink, a bottle of Charles Heidseick Champagne and a bottle of Stout, fill the glass one half full with Stout, the balance with Champagne, stir up with a spoon slowly, and you have what is called Champagne Velvet, because it will make you feel within a short time as fine as silk, it is rather an expensive drink, but a good one.

BACARDI STRAIGHT

A small wine-glass of BACARDI, before or after meals, produces a gentle heat in the stomach and favors digestion.

BACARDI COCKTAIL

A small wine-glass of BACARDI, the juice of half a lime, one or two teaspoonfuls of sugar, in a glass filled with ice, shake well, strain and serve.

BACARDI DUBONNET COCKTAIL

One half jigger BACARDI, one half jigger Dubonnet, juice of half a lime, one teaspoonful of Grenadine syrup, in a glass filled with ice, shake well and serve.

BACARDI GRENADINE COCKTAIL

One jigger BACARDI, one tablespoonful of Grenadine syrup, juice of half a lime, in a glass filled with ice, shake well and serve in cocktail glass.

BACARDI VERMOUTH COCKTAIL

(*DRY*)

Half wine-glass of BACARDI, half wine-glass of French Vermouth, cracked ice, stir and serve.

BACARDI VERMOUTH COCKTAIL

(*SWEET*)

Half wine-glass of BACARDI, half wine-glass of Italian Vermouth, cracked ice, stir and serve.

BACARDI RICKEY

Wine-glass of BACARDI, juice of half a lime, one lump of ice, serve in high-ball glass, add ISUAN.

BACARDI HIGHBALL

Place a piece of ice in high-ball glass, BACARDI, according to taste, fill glass with ISUAN.

BACARDI MILK PUNCH

One glass hot milk, one tablespoonful of sugar, a pinch of grated nutmeg, the yolk of an egg, a jigger of BACARDI, beat up thoroughly the yolk of the egg with the sugar, add milk, BACARDI and nutmeg, mix it thoroughly, it is a delicious punch and a very nice beverage for colds.

Classic Cocktail Guides and Retro Bartender Books

BACARDI GROG

Two quarts of BACARDI, two pounds of sugar, two quarts of Formosa Oolong tea, use the grog, adding equal part of very hot water, serve with slices of lemon, dissolve sugar in the hot water.

BACARDI BLOSSOM

(For Six Cocktails)

Four cocktail glasses of BACARDI, four teaspoonfuls of sugar, the juice of one orange, the juice of half a lime (or lemon), a little grated nutmeg, cracked ice, mix the sugar, orange and lime juice, a piece of orange and lime peel, grated nutmeg and cracked ice in the cocktail shaker and shake well to dissolve the sugar, then add BACARDI and some more ice if necessary. Shake vigorously again and serve.—Delicious!

BACARDI PEACH

Teaspoonful of powdered sugar, dissolve in water, crush fresh mint, juice of two lemons, three jiggers of BACARDI, layer of fine cracked ice, then one whole pitted fresh peach, another layer of fine cracked ice, dress with mint leaves, serve in tall glass with straws.

INDEX

HENRI DARVOIT
SPARKLING BURGUNDY

Made, Bottled,
and Aged
in France, the
Home
of Sparkling
Wines.

Henri Darvoit
Sparkling
Burgundy

will enhance the delight-
fulness of any Dinner
Party or Banquet.

KUENZLE & STREIFF, Inc.
SOLE DISTRIBUTORS

PHONE 113   343 T. PINPIN

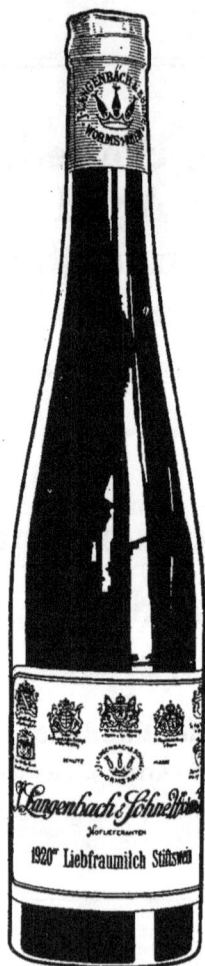

Classic Cocktail Guides and Retro Bartender Books

Alhambra Cigars

Leaders
Always

Coronas de la Alhambra
Half-a-Corona
Excelentes
Especiales
Bellezas
Presidentes Sumatra

Alhambra Cigar & Cigarette
Manufacturing Co.
Manila

Imitated but never equalled!

ISUAN DRY

Pale Ginger Ale

Quality
Supreme

Beck's Beer

IF YOU WOULD HAVE THE BEST GERMAN BEER
BREWED, ASK FOR BECK'S

KUENZLE & STREIFF, INC.

SOLE DISTRIBUTORS

PHONE 113   343 T. PINPIN

Historic Cookbooks of the World

Classic Cocktail Guides and Retro Bartender Books

Classic Cocktail Resource Guide

Some ingredients found in vintage cocktail guides are unavailable or hard to come by today. However, the creation of historically accurate cocktails is a growing hobby and with a bit of Internet research, you will find recipes for bitters and syrups online, as well as manufacturers that are developing new product lines for the classic cocktail enthusiast.

Vendors

A short selection of online vendors selling bitters, mixers, syrups, wine, liqueurs, and spirits. This list is by no means complete but is a good place to start your search.

BevMo!
www.bevmo.com

Binny's Beverage Depot
www.binnys.com

The Bitter Truth
www.the-bitter-truth.com

Cocktail Kingdom
www.cocktailkingdom.com

Fee Brothers
www.feebrothers.com

Hi-Time Wine Cellars
www.hitimewine.net

Internet Wines and Spirits
www.internetwines.com

The Jug Shop
www.thejugshop.com

Monin Gourmet Flavorings
www.moninstore.com

Trader Tiki's Hand-Crafted Exotic Syrups
www.tradertiki.com

The Whiskey Exchange
www.thewhiskyexchange.com

General Interest

*These sites provide background information on individual ingredients,
suggestions for substitutes, current commercial availability, and recipes.*

The Chanticleer Society
A Worldwide Organization of Cocktail Enthusiasts
www.chanticleersociety.org

Drink Boy
Adventures in Cocktails
www.drinkboy.com

The Internet Cocktail Database Ingredients Search
www.cocktaildb.com/ingr_search

Museum of the American Cocktail
www.museumoftheamericancocktail.org

WebTender Wiki
www.wiki.webtender.com

Now Available from Classic Cocktail Guides
and Retro Bartender Books

Stuart's Fancy Drinks
and How to Mix Them

Containing Clear and Practical Directions for
Mixing All Kinds of Cocktails, Sours, Egg Nog,
Sherry Cobblers, Coolers, Absinthe, Crustas,
Fizzes, Flips, Juleps, Fixes, Punches, Lemonades,
Pousse Cafes, Invalids' Drinks, Etc. Etc.

Thomas Stuart

ISBN: 978-1-880954-34-8

Jack's Manual of Recipes for Fancy Mixed Drinks and How to Serve Them

A Pre-Prohibition Cocktail Book

J. A. Grohusko

ISBN: 978-1-880954-28-7

Now Available from Classic Cocktail Guides
and Retro Bartender Books

The Twentieth-Century Guide for Mixing Fancy Drinks

A Pre-Prohibition Cocktail Book

James C. Maloney

ISBN: 978-1-880954-29-4

The Ideal Bartender

Cocktails and Mixed Drinks
from the Years of the First World War

Tom Bullock
Bartender of the Pendennis Club, Louisville, Kentucky
and of the St. Louis Country Club

Introduction by George H. Walker
Grandfather to President George Herbert Walker Bush
and Great-Grandfather to President George Walker Bush

ISBN: 978-1-880954-31-7

Nineteenth-Century Cocktail Creations

How to Mix Drinks: A Bar Keeper's Handbook

George Winter

ISBN: 978-1-880954-30-0

Now Available from Classic Cocktail Guides
and Retro Bartender Books

Daly's Bartenders' Encyclopedia

A Pre-Prohibition Cocktail Book

Tim Daly

ISBN: 978-1-880954-32-4

Coming Soon from
Classic Cocktail Guides
and Retro Bartender Books

Home Made Beverages

The Manufacture of Non-Alcoholic and
Alcoholic Drinks in the Household, Including
Recipes for Essences, Extracts, and Syrups

A Pre-Prohibition Cocktail Book

Albert Hopkins

www.ingramcontent.com/pod-product-compliance
Lightning Source LLC
Chambersburg PA
CBHW021144020426
42331CB00005B/893